Simon Schrock

Your
STRENGTH
CAN BECOME YOUR
WEAKNESS

WITH STUDY QUESTIONS

Your Strength Can Become Your Weakness

ISBN: 0-940883-23-6

NOTE: Names in the illustrations are fictitious, but they represent real life situations.

For additional copies or comments, contact

Simon Schrock

Choice Books of NVA

10100 Piper Lane

Bristow, VA 20136

Printed By:

8757 County Road 77

Fredericksburg, Ohio 44627

P. 888-473-6870

TABLE OF CONTENTS

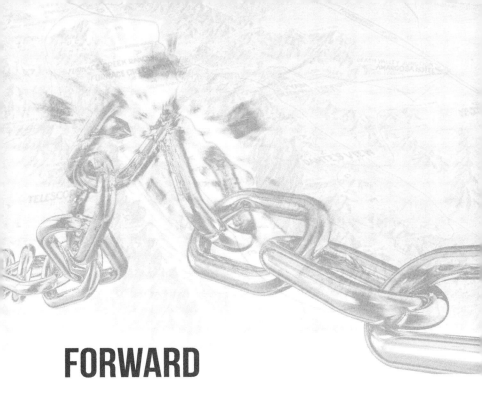

FORWARD

Sometimes it's difficult to recognize when things are up-side down. We become accustomed to what we believe to be the right perspective. The artist may view things differently than the observer. He understands what he is painting or forming, and knows the message that he wants to convey through his work. Sometimes the observer is left to wonder. The casual observer will view the creator and the creation of the kingdom of Heaven in a similar manner. Do kingdom principles really make sense? Is humility really the way up? Does pride really go before a fall? Is being a servant really the way to greatness?

The concepts taught in this book are based on the upside down teachings of our great Rabbi Jesus Christ. These are Kingdom principles. These principles are upside down as compared to those taught by the world's kingdom. In God's kingdom the least is the greatest, the weak are strong, the guilty find innocence, the mature become as children, and the "righteous" miss the feast; however, the poor, the maimed, the halt, and the blind are gathered to the great supper. In the same manner then, can we say that the weak are strong and the strong are weak? It is certainly possible as Schrock points out, that this does occur.

In writing about what makes some companies good and others great, Jim Collins in Good to Great states, "A great organization is one that makes a distinctive impact and delivers superior performance over a long period of time." Jim makes the case that what keeps many organizations from becoming great is the fact that they are good. A struggling organization may see the need of getting help and consequently becomes better. However, a good organization may feel that its performance is acceptable, and so it fails to ever achieve the status of greatness. Why? Because its strength has become its weakness! They have become satisfied with the status quo- with being good.

The Pharisee was delighted that he was not as "other" men are. After all, he was not greedy, or unjust, or an adulterer, or even as this collector of public revenue. He fasted twice a week and tithed of all his income. He did things the right way! He was a good man! In fact he was so good that he had need of nothing. However, this man's strength was his undoing. His goodness caused his pride, arrogance and self-righteousness. He needed no help or justification, and unless he changed his view he would receive none. In the end, this likely cost him eternal life!

The "other" man, however, recognized his weakness, insufficiency, and sinfulness. This caused him to humbly beg for mercy and forgiveness, and thus he was justified. His weakness became his strength!

Schrock notes that "Many believers stumble and fall over their strengths and not their weaknesses. Some Christians are limited in their effectiveness and usefulness through their strengths." He suggests that we offend each other more with our strengths than with our weaknesses.

A.W. Tozer says it this way. "There are areas in our lives where in our effort to be right we may go wrong, in our determination to be bold we become brazen, in our desire to be frank we become rude, in our effort to be watchful we become suspicious, when we seek to be serious we become somber, and when we mean to be conscientious we become over-scrupulous." These areas all seem to illustrate a strength becoming a weakness.

Is it possible to become aware of our weakness and work on strengthening those areas of life, while at the same time failing to recognize that our strengths are or could become our greatest areas of weakness? Perhaps many of us have not considered the fact that our strength may actually be where we have a weakness- a weakness that causes problems in our relationship with Christ and our fellowmen.

As based on God's Word, the book you are reading teaches us balance. It allows us to examine our lives- to see where our blind spots are. Schrock's life and ministry experiences have given him a unique insight into the strengths and weaknesses within relationships. With the aid of the Spirit, allow your mind to be illuminated to see where your strengths may have become weaknesses.

Bill Mullet

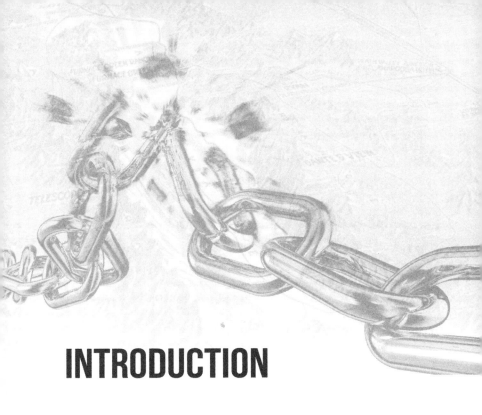

INTRODUCTION

Reading through the Bible yearly is a journey of encouraging and exciting events of God at work in past history and His promises for the future. It gives the believer guidance for living now and promises a most blessed, eternal future. The repeated journey through the Bible shows how God's plan is carried on through His faithful followers.

In the book of Exodus Moses recorded specific instructions he received from God for building the tabernacle and its appurtenances. As I read these detailed instructions, I wonder how a person could possibly fulfill God's requirement in this momentous task. Then reading further, the answer to my wondering is made clear in Exodus 31. God called certain persons to take responsibility to carry out His divine orders. He gave them His Spirit and ability to understand and know how to build according to His "blueprint." Moses wrote and explained how a miracle team, working for God, would accomplish His commandments.

> "And the Lord spake unto Moses, saying, See, I have called by name Bezaleel the son of Uri, the son of Hur, of the tribe of Judah: And I have filled him with the Spirit of God, in wisdom, and in understanding, and in knowledge, and in all manner of workmanship, To devise cunning works, to work in gold, and in silver, and in brass, And in cutting of stones, to set them, and in carving of timber, to work in all manner of workmanship. And I, behold, I have given with him Aholiab, the son of Ahisamach, of the tribe of Dan: and in the hearts of all that are wise hearted I have put wisdom, that they may make all that I have commanded thee;" (Exodus 31:1-6).

God called Bezaleel, filled him with His Spirit, and gave him a special helper named Aholiab. In addition to these two chosen and called persons, He gave wisdom to the hearts of those who are wise, and the ability to "make all that I have commanded." God gave this team a special skill to make all the furnishings of the Tabernacle which included the gold lampstand with all its accessories, the incense altar, and the altar of burnt offerings. They made the sacred garments for Aaron, the high priest, and his sons to wear as they ministered in their priestly duties.

It is a thrill to see how God worked over thousands of years to bring us "good tidings of great joy, which shall be to all people. For unto you is born this day in the city of David a Saviour which is Christ the Lord" (Luke 2:10-11).

Does God still give gifts of wisdom, understanding and knowledge to His dedicated followers today? Does God still use people in shaping events and history for another "good news" climax, the coming again of Jesus to take His bride to Himself and His new tabernacle?

In my journey through the Bible, I find encouraging and exciting promises that God is still working His plan through His people. God performed miraculous works during the period of the covenant of the law. God's marvelous works continue through today's covenant of grace. He gives His followers His Spirit with various gifts "for the work of the ministry" in guiding His people today. He gives gifts of insight to steer us through what Jesus called an "adulterous and sinful generation" (Mark 8:38), and the "perilous times" that the Apostle Paul warned "shall come." (See 2 Timothy 3:1-13).

God inspired Paul to compare the functions of the human body to how God works today in His body, the church.

As you read the following passage from I Corinthians 12:18 through 27, let your thoughts fathom the beauty of God's people functioning in the body of the church.

"But now hath God set the members every one of them in the body, as it hath pleased him. And if they were all one member, where were the body? But now are they many members, yet but one body. And the eye cannot say unto the hand, I have no need of thee: nor again the head to the feet, I have no need of you. Nay, much more those members of the body, which seem to be more feeble, are necessary: And those members of the body, which we think to be less honourable, upon these we bestow more abundant honour; and our uncomely parts have more abundant comeliness. For our comely parts have no need: but God hath tempered the body together, having given more abundant honour to that part which lacked: That there should be no schism in the body; but that the members should have the same care one for another. And whether one member suffer, all the members suffer with it; or one member be honoured, all the members rejoice with it. Now ye are the body of Christ, and members in particular."

If you are a born-again believer you are a temple in which the Spirit of God dwells and you are part of Christ's body. "Now ye are the body of Christ." This means you have a gift to help build up the body of Christ. Think of that! God has a purpose for you to fulfill in His church.

In the Old Testament era, God called His people into a team to build the tabernacle and all its furnishings. In the New Testament era He gives His disciples spiritual gifts to team together in fulfilling His plan until "the tabernacle of God will be with men, and he will dwell with them, and they shall be his people, and God himself shall be with them and be their God" (Revelation 21:3).

"Your Strength Can Become Your Weakness" is presented with the hope and prayer that members of the church will team together in using their various gifts to expand and maintain the kingdom of God. God filled Bezaleel with His spirit and gave him wisdom, understanding and knowledge. Paul's prayer for Colossian Christians is ideal for believers today. "We . . . do not cease to pray for you, and to desire that ye might be filled with the knowledge of his will in all wisdom and spiritual understanding" (Colossians 1:9).

Will you be committed to exercising your gift to the glory of God until He comes in the twinkling of an eye or calls you home to His eternal tabernacle?

- Simon Schrock
March 19, 2015

chapter 1

YOUR STRENGTH CAN BECOME YOUR WEAKNESS

Do you remember helping your grandmother with washing clothes, or cleaning the kitchen, and seeing the Borax box of detergent with a picture of the famous 20 mule team? "20 MULE TEAM borax boasts the cleaning power of your detergent. It helps to remove soil and stains, brightens clothes, and freshens your laundry."

Borax deposits were discovered in Death Valley in 1873. Actual mining began in the early 1880's with 20 mule teams. Teams of 20 mules in each team hauled the Borax out of Death Valley. From there it moved to the shelves of grocery stores and then into Grandma's kitchen. First appearing in history over 4000 years ago, borax remains in use today because it's so effective and versatile.

Death Valley lies in east Central California, near the Nevada border. It is a deep trough about 130 miles long and from 6-14 miles wide. At the center point it is 282 feet below sea level.

Rainfall averages about 2 inches a year. The summer temperatures of 125 degrees Fahrenheit are common. The highest temperature ever recorded in the United States was 134 degrees in 1913.

Imagine the teamwork it took to get a team of 20 mules to haul loads of Borax "up out of there" in 125 degree weather. In such a setting 20 mules had to work together to get a job done.

Suppose with me a man named George drove on of these teams. And in the team was a mule named Rex. Rex was an outstanding contribution to the team. He was exceptionally strong. When George cries out "Getty-up," Rex starts and they all begin to pull. After a while, Rex gets impatient with the other 19, the weaker 19. He begins to really dig in and pull. He shows his strength full force. But the other 19 become disoriented. Some pull to the right, some to the left, and some balk. Rex's strength becomes his weakness.

That is what this message is about. "Your strength can become your weakness."

Romans 14:1 "Him that is weak in the faith, receive ye but not to doubtful disputations." Do not perplex him with your continuing discussions or pass judgment.

Romans 15:1 "We then that are strong ought to bear the infirmities of the weak, and not to please ourselves." Who is weak? Who is strong?

If these verses were part of a Sunday class discussion, you might hear comments like "they," "the weaker they," etc, with reference to someone other than the person speaking.

It could be that those who think they are strong are actually weak. Those who think they are weak may be the stronger. After all, it was the Lord who told the Apostle Paul, "My grace is sufficient for thee, for my strength is made perfect in weakness" (2 Corinthians 12:9).

Many believers stumble and fall over their strengths and not their weaknesses. Some Christians are limited in their effectiveness and usefulness through their strengths. I suggest that we offend each other more with our strengths than with our weaknesses.

Someone has said, "Success has made failures of many men." Christians are members of Christ's body. "Now you are Christ's body, and individually members of it" (1 Corinthians 12:27 NAS). The Bible referred to the "weak" and the "strong." It is His design that they pull together in building up His body."

In Romans 12, God's Word gives us a "seven gift team" for pulling together in the work of Christ and his church.

> "For just as we have many members in one body and all the members do not have the same function, so we, who are many, are one body in Christ, and individually members one of another. Since we have gifts that differ according to the grace given to us, each of us is to exercise them accordingly: if prophecy, according to the proportion of his faith; if service, in his serving; or he who teaches, in his teaching; or he who exhorts, in his exhortation; he who gives, with liberality; he who leads, with diligence; he who shows mercy, with cheerfulness" (Romans 12:4-8 NAS).

Next notice the purpose of being teamed together.

> "And He gave some as apostles, and some as prophets, and some as evangelists, and some as pastors and teachers, for the equipping of the saints for the work of service, to the building up of the body of Christ; until we all attain to the unity of the faith, and of the knowledge of the Son of God, to a mature man, to the measure of the stature which belongs to the fullness of Christ. As a result, we are no longer to be children, tossed here and there by waves and carried about by every wind of doctrine, by the trickery of men, by craftiness in deceitful scheming" (Ephesians 4:11-14 NAS).

What are some of the reasons for the different gifts working together?

+ Perfecting the saints
+ Edifying the body
+ Unity of faith
+ Knowledge of the Son of God
+ Come to fullness in Christ

Steadfast, not shifting to and fro. (Not like a sign in a pretzel shop, "All kinds of twisting and turning done here." That sign would fit into many churches.)

We are given gifts for very noble purposes.

"But speaking the truth in love, we are to grow up in all aspects into Him who is the head, even Christ, from whom the whole body, being fitted and held together by what every joint supplies, according to the proper working of each individual part, causes the growth of the body for the building up of itself in love" (Ephesians 4:15-16 NAS).

+ Speaking the truth in love
+ Building each other up in love
+ Coming together in oneness
+ Knowing Jesus better

chapter 2

LET'S GET INTO THE TEAM

Now; let's get "teamed up" and see how we are to use our gifts to pull together. I'll take the Romans 12 team of seven and add one from Ephesians 4 to make an eight gift team.

Remember the 20 mule team pulled together to bring Borax up out of Death Valley.

Remember seeing four horse teams in Lancaster County PA, pulling a farm implement preparing the field for planting? God designed for believers to pull together in planting and harvesting.

This illustration may help you catch the vision of teaming up and exercising your gift in pulling together.

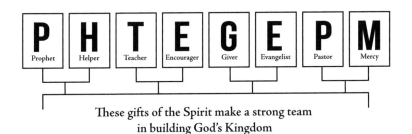

These gifts of the Spirit make a strong team
in building God's Kingdom

This eight gift team has names. Their names represent their gifts or their strengths.

1) The Prophet.

A spokesman for God to man.

The prophet can clearly say, "Thus saith the Lord." Proclaiming the Word and will of God.

The prophet warns and exhorts.

The prophet might be quick to say, "You need to repent now."

The prophet may be strongly convinced of being right on the issue.

2) The Helper

Ability to serve behind the scene.

Encouraging and strengthening others.

Takes the trash out without being asked if it helps the cause.

Cheerfully giving a helping hand where needed without expecting a lot of credit from others.

Ready to do anything, even make coffee for others.

3) The Teacher

A keen interest in the personal study of the Word of God.

Is disciplined in studying the Scriptures.

The teacher will not have a plaque on the desk with a quote from Ecclesiastes 12:12, "And much study is weariness of the flesh."

Willing to show and explain how to do a task.

4) The Encourager

Helping others pursue, or do what the teacher taught.

Calling to one's side and giving aid.

Looks for ways to affirm others.

5) The Giver

The capacity to give to the work of the Lord consistently, liberally, sacrificially, and with wisdom.

Gives with cheerfulness so that others are encouraged and blessed.

Enjoys supporting the Church by giving.

Willingly supports mission outreach work.

6) *The Evangelist*

The capacity to present the gospel message with the exceptional clarity and overwhelming burden.

Passionate about the "good news" reaching others.

7) *Pastor-Ruler*

God given capacity to organize and administer.

Administrates with efficiency and spirituality, so as to bring the project to a satisfactory conclusion with harmony and God's blessings.

Ready to walk with others in their struggles.

Has an understanding love and sympathy for people dealing with serious illness and death in the family.

Cares deeply about the pain others are experiencing.

8) *Mercy*

Compassion for the miserable and hurting.

The ability to give acts of mercy that are undeserved by the other.

Mercy might say, "I feel your pain," and cry with the suffering and mistreated.

Notice something very interesting in the Romans 12 team. Prophet is on one end, mercy on the other. The prophet wants to solve the problem right away and get on to something else. Mercy wants to hang in until the last ember of hope is gone. The prophet will pull the plug of life support while mercy still holds on for a possible miracle.

The prophet will have a measure of the other gifts, but will be most comfortable being a prophet. The helper may have a measure of other gifts, but is most comfortable being a helper or server. The same principle applies to all the gifts.

A plaque that was a gift to me hangs on my office wall. It boldly declares;

"TEAM, Together Everyone Achieves More". This reminds me of the prayer of Jesus to the Father on behalf of "them which thou hast given me; for they are mine".

> "That they may be one; as thou, Father, art in me, and I in thee, that they also may be one in us: that the world may believe that thou hast sent me. And the glory which thou gavest me I have given them; that they may be one, even as we are one; I in them, and thou in me, that they may be perfect in one; and that the world may know that thou has sent me ,and hast loved them, as thou hast loved me " (John 17: 21-23).

Different gifts working together on the same team is a strong witness to the unsaved world that Jesus is sent from God to save us from our sins.

chapter 3

GOD'S PLAN

Jack is a young husband and father. He is struggling with being faithful in his Christian life and marriage vow. Sometimes he feels like giving up and going with the world. As a result, his wife and young son suffer because he isn't experiencing victory and joy in the Lord as he should.

God's gift calls for team work.

Right now, Jack needs to experience merciful encouraging rebuke. What a combination of team work.

He needs to feel understood – mercy.

He needs to hear the facts – prophet.

He needs to want to change – encourager.

Sometimes it is difficult for one person to approach someone about the need to repent and change. If Brother Prophet goes to see Jack, he will likely exercise what comes easiest. He tells Jack in no uncertain terms, "You are not walking with the Lord as you should! And that's a fact! You better dot your spiritual 'I's' and get your spiritual comas in the right place – or else. Do you understand?"

Brother Prophet's strength of keenly forth telling the will of God becomes a weakness and discourages Jack. He doesn't realize that Jack's gift of giving doesn't automatically drink up the forceful, immediate demands of the prophet. The prophet is now ready to give the full force of discipline while the heat is on Jack to change.

Prophet – beware. Your strength can easily become your weakness. It becomes the greatest weakness when he doesn't help the team pull together in pulling Jack up out of Death Valley.

Now Mercy goes to see Jack. He is overwhelmed with compassion as he listens to Jack tell how he gave assistance to this woman where he works. (His strength of giving became his weakness when it went beyond simply giving to a needful woman.) Mercy concludes Jack has been wrongly accused. It is not his fault. Decisions his mother made while he was being formed or the discipline from his father when he was 10 had a direct influence on his behavior now. Mercy begins to sob with feelings of pain on Jacks behalf. And Jack almost worships mercy.

Showing compassion is a beautiful gift of the Holy Spirit. But the strength of mercy can become a weakness and a stumbling block. It becomes a weakness when it goes along with Jack's wrong way of living and does not call for correction or discipline. Mercy understands Jack's behavior, but doesn't press for change. It doesn't make a good team for pulling together to rescue Jack from Death Valley.

An ideal leadership team consists of the gift of a prophet coupled with mercy. Adding a measure of the pastor-ruler, encourager and teacher makes a balanced team to tackle Death Valley problems. A one-pastor or leader often lacks some of the gifts and insights required to lead a group to a satisfactory conclusion. This may also be the case when attempting to help a person trapped in a sin to turn to being fully committed to God.

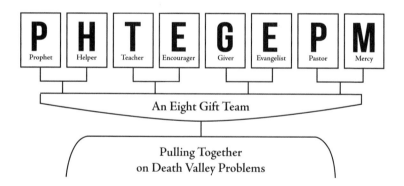

The leadership team (ministerial team) works on developing a statement of practice for daily living. The prophet is able to recall history and how certain decisions led to departure from the true faith. He can also visualize where certain decision will lead them. He will be cautious. Mercy tends to please the people.

Mercy doesn't want to offend anyone by asking for sacrifice for the sake of the other. What happened in history doesn't apply. A good conclusion needs input from both. Team leadership can be a beautiful gift from God.

The gifted team becomes a weakness when one gift insists on doing it his way without due consideration of the other gifts. The prophet's strengths may become weakness when he takes part of the church and starts another group with strict law and order. He may soon have more order than he bargained for as he finds his flock dwindling to a few other like-minded prophets.

Mercy's strength becomes weakness when patience runs thin with the prophet's constant emphasis on defending the faith, and throws in the towel to start another church. His focus is on just following the leading of the Spirit. Mercy may soon have a large following with little order and discipline and questionable doctrine.

Someone has said, "Mercy and truth must walk hand in hand. Mercy without truth excuses. Truth without mercy crushes."

The prophet enjoys sermons by other prophets. Like-minded prophets will hold him in high esteem. Mercy absorbs mercy sermons. Mercy is viewed as having charisma and influencing large numbers of people. A balanced position can be helpful in faithfully guiding God's people through a sinful and adulterous generation.

chapter 4

BEWARE LEST SATAN GETS AN ADVANTAGE

In Paul's second letter to the Corinthian Church he drew attention to someone among them who had caused them grief. He admonished them that the punishment inflicted on such a man was sufficient, and now they ought to forgive and confirm their love toward him, "Lest Satan should get an advantage of us: for we are not ignorant of devices" (2 Corinthians 2:11). The Apostle also reminds us that "Satan himself is transformed into an angel of light. Therefore it is no great thing if his ministers also be transformed as ministers of righteousness, whose end shall be according to their works" (2 Corinthians 11:14-15). "Lest Satan should get an advantage". Satan not only seeks to take advantage of the believers weakness, but also attempt to "get an advantage" of their strengths. Strengths are sometimes gained in the way we were trained through childhood. A husband may feel the way he was raised is the only right way. His wife's way of being trained may also be right. While they may both be right, their insistence in being right may become a weakness where Satan can get an advantage.

Luke gave the account of Jesus' visit in Martha's home. She demonstrated her strength of hospitable serving. While her service is a remarkable strength, she missed a needed part of Jesus' visit. Is there a lesson here for believers today?

> "Now it came to pass, as they went, that he entered into a certain village: and a certain woman named Martha received him into her house. And she had a sister called Mary, which also sat at Jesus' feet, and heard his word. But Martha was cumbered about much serving, and came to him, and said, Lord, dost thou not care that my sister hath left me to serve alone? bid her therefore that she help me. And Jesus answered and said unto her, Martha, Martha, thou art careful and troubled about many things: But one thing is needful: and Mary hath chosen that good part, which shall not be taken away from her" (Luke 10:38-42).

In a daily devotional, "How To Launch Your Day", Albert Epp reflects on Jesus' visit to Martha's house.

"Jesus stopped at Martha's house at Bethany, on the eastern slope of the Mount of Olives. Apparently, Mary lived with her sister. But clearly Martha was the predominant person. It was her house. She is the hostess. She welcomes Christ. The welcome mat was always out for Jesus and His disciples.

Martha was busy in the kitchen, Mary chose to sit at Jesus' feet. The Canadian scholar, E. Earl Ellis, writes, ". . . the story reflects a dinner scene, as was the custom. Jesus reclined on his side at the table. Mary . . . sat at the Lord's feet. The picture is that of a Rabbi instructing his pupil . . . Judaism did not forbid women to be instructed in the Torah, but it was unusual for a Rabbi to lower himself to this."

Martha, working alone in the kitchen became upset. She obviously had the spiritual gifts of Hospitality and Service. Jesus gently rebuked her. Mary's gifts are harder to discern. Some suggest Teaching and Exhortation. At any rate, Jesus praised Mary for her choice! We all need to guard against allowing our busyness to crowd out our quality time with Christ. And further, we should refrain from criticizing people with gifts different from ours!"

Martha was worried and troubled over many things, giving Satan an advantage in keeping her from "that good part, which shall not be taken away from her". Christians can become so deeply engrossed in exercising their strong gift that they become too busy to sit at Jesus' feet and hear His Word.

Sue grew up in a home where manners, quietness, and expressing love was a strong point. It was a definite strength. She was accustomed to hearing her parents say, "I love you," "Have a good trip," and "Thank you for helping." She even got a thank you note from her brother. Closeness with family was her strength. She married Jack. He never heard his father say, "I love you," "You did a good job," or "thank you for helping me."

Jack's impression of love was meeting her necessities of life – providing money for groceries, taking her to see the doctor when she was about to give birth to their child, pay all the bills, and not chase other women. This included coming home for supper on time and not going "coon hunting" with the guys more than twice a month. He thought he dearly loved her.

After several years in the marriage, she felt unloved – and told him so. They got into quarrels, "You don't love me," "Of course I do, see these groceries?" She could not believe Jack loved her. She went to her pastor and the local psychiatrist and none of them could get Jack to love her. Sue's strength (mercy) of expressing love became such a weakness that she could not identify with Jack's way of saying, "I love you." Jack's strength of doing his duty (prophet) became such a weakness that he could not feel with Sue's emotions. Both their strengths became their weakness, and gave Satan an advantage. They could not pull each other out of this Death Valley rut.

Bill had the gift of giving. His gift was to earn and give. He was taught sound financial principles and programmed them into his life. Several other members of the church just didn't seem to make it. Bill knows about it and gives them a scathing lecture. He can't see how they can be good members and not be financially successful and live like he does. They become discouraged and find another church. That broke up the team and gave Satan an advantage. Bill's strength became his weakness.

Joseph, the prophet, raised six children successfully. They all turned out "all right." That was a strength. But he simply could not empathize with the father who had openly rebellious children. His strength gave him superior status in the church and community. But his inability to understand others (mercy) with their problems caused others to feel inferior around him. They couldn't team up with him and find help and strength. His strength became weakness when he couldn't team up with others and help them.

Marie was a very particular house keeper. Her spotless houses reflected her gifted neatness. For years, she nagged her husband, "Put your hat here, and don't ever kick your shoes there." What she said was the rule of the house, and he had to walk the line. That is, if he wanted any peace around the house. Neatness was her strength. But her husband slowly withdrew. He thought, "I don't count around here." They went from a fun couple to be with to just trying to peacefully co-exist. She had a conspicuously neat house, but a frustrated withdrawn husband, which gave Satan an advantage. Her strength became the undoing of a good relationship.

Jerry was a very detailed and demanding employer. He kept a close eye on everyone. Things had to be just like he wanted them. His strength was to think through everything with a presumed outcome. That was his strong gift – until he pushed so hard his employees became frustrated and couldn't produce at full pace. They felt like non-persons. His preciseness drove them away and they were no longer on the team.

Tom is a manager with a Master's Degree, which has led to management jobs in various companies. He has the resemblance of a prophet who can give orders with the air that it's "my way or the highway." He is hired to reverse the direction of a company sliding toward "death valley." But he has not yet learned to team with the other gifts on the team in his department. Because of his strength, he does not see or understand the caution lights flashing by the helper, the giver, or mercy. The entire department slides the organization closer to Death Valley. What appeared to be a strength became a weakness.

Ellis is a young I.T.(Information Technology) expert. He lives by his Smart Phone, relies on his lap top, travels by GPS and stays in contact with Facebookers. When he is at meetings he constantly slips in some texting. He keeps watching some gadget he has in his hand. So much so that he misses some of the real questions at hand. Jake has reached the three score and ten years in life. He has found it difficult to adapt to this new world of technology. He does have a good grasp on the teaching of Scripture and history. He has some concerns where following the new way of life will lead us. He would have some good advise for the technology "freak", but really hearing each other is a challenge. Both have some gifted strengths that contribute to weakness.

Be aware of this, the devil targets us at the point of our giftedness and strength. Judas was the treasurer for the band of Jesus' disciples. He must have had a portion of management gifts. He was the keeper of the money bag. Matthew reports an incident of his weakness.

> "And when Jesus was in Bethany at the house of Simon the leper, woman came to Him having an alabaster flask of very costly fragrant oil, and she poured it on His head as He sat at the table. But when His disciples saw it, they were indignant, saying, "Why this waste? For this fragrant oil might have been sold for much and given to the poor."

> But when Jesus was aware of it, He said to them, "Why do you trouble the woman? For she has done a good work for Me. For you have the poor with you always, but Me you do not have always. For in pouring this fragrant oil on My body, she did it for My burial. Assuredly, I say to you, wherever this gospel is preached

in the whole world, what this woman has done will also be told as a memorial to her" (Matthew 6:26-13).

John identifies that Judas Iscariot asked the question why this precious ointment was not sold and given to the poor.

> But one of His disciples, Judas Iscariot, Simon's son, who would betray Him, said, "Why was this fragrant oil not sold for three hundred denarii and given to the poor?" (John 12:4-5)

Judas saw the money. Jesus saw the person. Judas' over-concern for the finances caused him to miss the wonder and beauty of the occasion. When the woman anointed the feet of Jesus with costly ointment, He saw the wasted ointment but not the wonder of the worship.

Strengths can become weakness. As Cedric B. Johnson wrote,

"A conscientious person may become compulsive.

A giving person may take too much responsibility for others.

An open-hearted person may become gullible.

A discerning person may become skeptical.

We need to beware that the place of our strength does not become the stage on which Satan acts out this evil drama"[1]

Oswald Chambers makes this point "Unguarded strength is double weakness. The Bible characters fall on their strong point, never on their weakness."[2]

---

1 *Channeling Your Passions*, 1985. Person to Person Books, page 49
2 *My Utmost for His Highest*, Barbour and Co.

SO WHAT SHALL WE DO?

If unguarded strength becomes weakness how shall a person guard against it?

1. Take heed.

Be aware of tripping over your own strength. I Corinthians 10:12 is a reminder, "Wherefore let him that thinketh he standeth take heed lest he fall."

Romans 11:20b reminds us, "Be not highminded, but fear" "So do not become proud and conceited, but rather stand in awe and be reverently afraid." (Amplified)

Take heed and be aware of the fact that your strength may cause discord in the team. Your strength may actually become a hindrance in Death Valley rescue efforts.

Relationships are priority with God. That involves our relationship with Him first, and then our relationship with others. Jesus said to him, "'You shall love the Lord your God with all your heart, with all your soul, and with all your mind.' This is the first and great commandment. And the second is like it: 'You shall love your neighbor as yourself.' On these two commandments hang all the Law and the Prophets" (Matthew 22:37-40).

Take heed, lest the way you exercise you strength destroys good relationships (remember spotless Marie, a spotless clean house, but a lousy marriage.) Sometimes it is better to give up the argument than lose the relationship.

2. Balance your intake

"Every word of God is pure" (Proverbs 30:5). It is not unusual to read and reread your favorite passages of Scripture. One person may be absorbed in doctrine, another in the practical, another in the prophetical, and another in the experimental. Our conduct should make it clear that this is not the right way to study.

The "doctrinist" becomes loose in practice. The practical become self-righteous in principle. The prophetic disciple neglects present obligations. The experimental may mistake religion to be a feeling or excitement.

We tend to read what we like and what meshes easiest with our giftedness. That can be a strength. However, it can become a weakness when we read what we like at the expense of what we need.

I was reminded of my need to balance my reading by another member of the church, Stephen Russell. The challenge took me to read the 1,070 page "Complete Writings of Menno Simons." That makes it a one-year project of 3 pages a day. It took me a long time to read J.C. Wenger's "Introduction to Theology." I read it, because I needed it.

A balanced reading diet includes what you like as well as what you need, even though it takes more conscious effort to get through it.

Balanced reading starts with the Bible. For the one who enjoys the practical, balance it with history, theology, and season it with prophecy. The person who focuses on end-time events and has a clear view of how prophecy may be fulfilled should also focus on how to encourage others in the here and now.

3. Pull in the team

"Now concerning spiritual gifts, brethren, I do not want you to be ignorant... There are diversities of gifts, but the same Spirit. There are differences of ministries, but the same Lord. And there are diversities of activities, but it is the same God who works all in all. But the manifestation of the Spirit is given to each one for the profit of all...For as the body is one and has many members, but all the members of that one body, being many, are one body, so also is Christ. For by one Spirit we were all baptized into one body—whether Jews or Greeks, whether slaves or free—and have all been made to drink into one Spirit. For in fact the body is not one member but many...If the foot should say, "Because I am not a hand, I am not of the body," is it therefore not of the body? And if the ear should say, "Because I am not an eye, I am not of the body," is it therefore not of the body? If the whole body were an eye, where would be the hearing? If the whole were hearing, where would be the smelling? But now God has set the members, each one of them, in the body just as He pleased. And if they were all one member, where would the body be?...But now indeed there are many members, yet one body. And the eye cannot say to the hand, "I have no need of you"; nor again the head to the feet, "I have no need of you." No, much rather, those members of the body which seem to be weaker are necessary. And those members of the body which we think to be less honorable, on these we bestow greater honor; and our unpresentable parts have greater modesty...Now you are the body of Christ, and members individually" (Excerpts from 1 Corinthians 12).

Paul reminds us in his letter to the Corinthian believers that we are many members but one body. Different gifts, but one team.

Be a team worker. As Peter admonishes, "As each one has a special gift, employ it in serving one another, as good stewards of the manifold grace of God" (1 Peter 4;10, NAS).

When you take your strength and become independent it becomes a weakness. Your strength can often be best utilized in the team. Discerners need to team up with mercy, and mercy needs the insight of the discerner.

When you go on your own, it will tend to cut off others, insult them, and drive them away. Then in years to come, you may be a lonely loner, trying to put on a satisfied front. Our strengths are given to assist each other and not to make us independent individuals. As Peter wrote, "employ it in serving one another."

4. Team up in the Spirit of Christ.

Since you are encouraged by belonging in Christ and comforted by his love and enjoy the fellowship of the Spirit, then Philippians 2:1-8 becomes our guide.

> "If there be therefore any consolation in Christ, if any comfort of love, if any fellowship of the Spirit, if any bowels and mercies, Fulfil ye my joy, that ye be likeminded, having the same love, being of one accord, of one

mind. Let nothing be done through strife or vainglory; but in lowliness of mind let each esteem other better than themselves. Look not every man on his own things, but every man also on the things of others. Let this mind be in you, which was also in Christ Jesus: Who, being in the form of God, thought it not robbery to be equal with God: But made himself of no reputation, and took upon him the form of a servant, and was made in the likeness of men: And being found in fashion as a man, he humbled himself, and became obedient unto death, even the death of the cross."

Teaming up in the Spirit of Christ and working for the good of others makes a good team worker in rescuing souls from Death Valley.

5. *Present yourself to the King.*

The Bible declares that Jesus Christ is the King of kings. Every king and president will eventually confess that Jesus Christ is Lord. Having seen a number of U.S. presidents reminds me of a story from my mother. The crowd gathered to see the president in person. The little boy couldn't see him because of crowd. Dad lifted him up, likely on his shoulders. After seeing the president, the boy exclaimed (sel is yust a mon) "That's just a man."

"Therefore God also has highly exalted Him and given Him the name which is above every name, that at the name of Jesus every knee should bow, of those in heaven, and of those on earth, and of those under the earth" (Philippians 2:9-10).

Jesus is Lord. All people, including kings, will need to recognize He is LORD.

The "born again" believer is a child of the King. To use your gift to the utmost, commit yourself and your gift back to the King.

> "I beseech you therefore, brethren, by the mercies of God, that you present your bodies a living sacrifice, holy, acceptable to God, which is your reasonable service. And do not be conformed to this world, but be transformed by the renewing of your mind, that you may prove what is that good and acceptable and perfect will of God" (Romans 12:1-2).

In committing yourself to the King, you become His ambassador. "Now then, we are ambassadors for Christ" (2 Corinthians 5:20).

Commit yourself to the work in his team serving one another with love, as we are encouraged to do in Galatians 5:13-16 "For you, brethren, have been called to liberty; only do not use liberty as an opportunity for the flesh, but through love serve one another. For all the law is fulfilled in one word, even in this:

'You shall love your neighbor as yourself.' But if you bite and devour one another, beware lest you be consumed by one another! I say then: Walk in the Spirit, and you shall not fulfill the lust of the flesh"

Presenting yourself to the King will be helpful in preventing your strength from becoming your weakness.

The born again believer is the temple (dwelling place) of the Holy Spirit. The Spirits indwelling is accompanied by a useful gift to build up the disciples of Christ. Use your gift in service one to another.

Study
QUESTIONS

SPECIAL THANKS TO

Joe Miller (Ohio) and Jonas Lapp (Pennsylvania)

for contributed to the study questions

31

CHAPTER ONE
YOUR STRENGTH CAN BECOME YOUR WEAKNESS
(Including questions from Forward & Introduction)

- In the Forward is the example of the Pharisee who saw his righteousness as a strength. Was it a strength?
- If not, how did it become a weakness? How did the Publican's weakness become his strength?
- Does God still give gifts of wisdom, understanding and wisdom to His dedicated followers today?
- What causes believers to stumble over their strengths?
- According to Scripture, what are some of the purposes accomplished by teamwork?

notes: _____

_____

_____

_____

_____

_____

_____

_____

CHAPTER TWO
LET'S GET INTO THE TEAM

- What are the benefits of teaming up and pulling together?
- How is unity a witness to the unsaved world?
- How does the"mule spirit" - insisting having your own way - as a leader, affect the under shepherds? Or the sheep?
- How does lack of team spirit affect the brotherhood? How is lack of team spirit a detriment to growth?

notes: _____

_____

_____

_____

_____

_____

_____

_____

CHAPTER THREE
GOD'S PLAN

- How can one's strength become a stumbling block to others?
- When is singular leadership detrimental?
- How is team leadership beneficial?
- How can mercy and truth walk hand in hand?
- How can prophet and mercy strengthen each other?

notes: _____

_____

_____

_____

_____

_____

_____

_____

_____

CHAPTER FOUR
BEWARE LEST SATAN GETS AND ADVANTAGE

- Did Martha's gift of hospitality keep her from needful fellowship with Jesus?
- How does Satan take advantage of our strengths?
- How can our strength break up the team?
- Has Satan made inroads into our lives and churches by misuses of our gifts? If so, how?
- How can the convenient, fast paced era of IT (Information Technology) become a weakness?

notes: _____

_____

_____

_____

_____

_____

_____

_____

CHAPTER FIVE
SO WHAT SHALL WE DO?

- What can be done to counteract our weakness - or, to prevent our strength from becoming weakness?
- How do our strengths and gifts become useful?
- What characteristic of Jesus made Him the best team worker?
- Why should our gifts be presented back to the King?
- How do we become blinded to the fact that our strengths have become a detriment to us?
- Is the servanthood mentality a daily part of our lives?

notes: _____

_____
_____
_____
_____
_____
_____
_____
_____

other books
BY SIMON SCHROCK

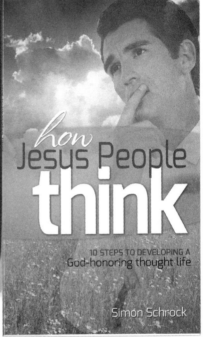

Don't Throw in the Towel
A Cyclorama of Encouragement!

How Jesus People Think
*10 steps to developing a God-honoring
thought life*

for more information, contact...
SIMON SCHROCK
10100 Piper Lane • Bristow, VA 20136

other books by

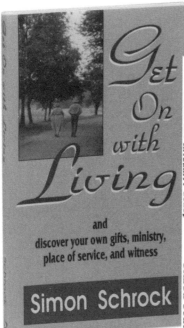

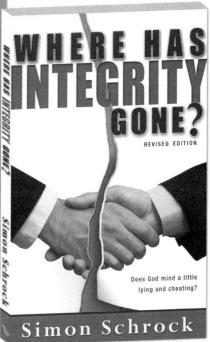

Get On with Living
*and discover your own gifts,
ministry, place of service,
and witness*

Where Has Integrity Gone?
Does God mind a little lying and cheating?

for more information, contact...
SIMON SCHROCK
10100 Piper Lane ◆ Bristow, VA 20136

Simon Schrock

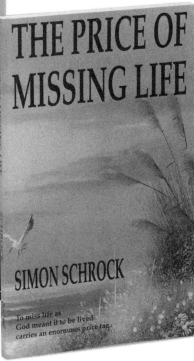

One Anothering
*It's time for a return to a simple,
practical lifestyle . . . getting along . . .
helping each other*

The Price of Missing Life
*To miss life as God meant it to be lived
carries an enormous price tag*

for more information, contact...

SIMON SCHROCK
10100 Piper Lane ✦ Bristow, VA 20136

other books by

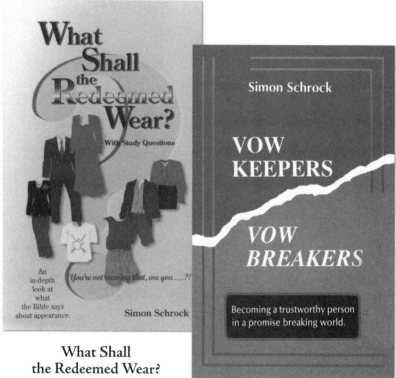

**What Shall
the Redeemed Wear?**
With Study Questions
*An in-depth look at what the Bible says
about appearance*

Vow Keepers Vow Breakers
*Becoming a trustworthy person
in a promise breaking world*

for more information, contact...
SIMON SCHROCK
10100 Piper Lane ◆ Bristow, VA 20136

Simon Schrock

A Smoother Journey
Keeping life's relationships out of the valleys and on the mountaintops

for more information, contact...
SIMON SCHROCK
10100 Piper Lane ✦ Bristow, VA 20136